Grandma Ellen and Me

Mabel R. Miller

Pacific Press® Publishing Association
Nampa, Idaho
Oshawa, Ontario, Canada

Edited by Jerry D. Thomas
Designed by Tim Larson
Cover and illustration art by Phyllis Pollema Cahill

Library of Congress Cataloging-in-Publication Data

Miller, Mabel R. (Mabel Robinson), 1910-
   Grandma Ellen and me : stories of growing up at Elmshaven/
   Mabel R. Miller.
      p. cm.
   Summary: The author shares memories and stories of growing
up with her great-grandmother Ellen, "a messenger for God."
     ISBN 978-0-8163-1691-5
   1. Miller, Mabel R. (Mabel Robinson), 1910- 2. White, Ellen Gould
Harmon, 1827-1915. [1. Miller, Mabel R. (Mabel Robinson), 1910-
2. White, Ellen Gould Harmon, 1827-1915. 3. Great-grandmothers.
4. Christian life.] I. Title.

   BX6193.M49 A3 2000
   286.7'092—dc21
   [B]

                         00-023953

May 2016

Contents

1

Little Brown House

When I was a little girl, I lived in a little brown house out in the country with my mother and father and my brother, Virgil. Our house was in the Napa Valley in California. In those days, the valley was filled with farms, ranches, and vineyards. I guess it still is.

Even though there weren't many other children living nearby, Virgil and I were never lonely. We had a big collie dog to play with and six cats who chased mice in the barn. The big black-and-white cow and her frisky calf were our friends too.

And we always had chickens. Our chickens didn't stay cooped up inside a pen all day. They wandered through the yard around the barn, scratching and pecking at the dirt and grass. Every day, they wanted to play hide-and-seek! At least, that's the way it seemed to me when a hen would slip under a bush or behind a stack of hay to lay her egg.

Some days, it was my turn to play the game with them. Mama would hand me the basket and say, "Mabel, see how many eggs you can find. Be careful—don't break any." Off I would go, peeking behind Daddy's boxes and under the wagon. All around the barn, I would find eggs in little rounded nests snuggled into the hay. Carefully, I would stack them in my basket.

One day I was holding up a warm brown egg to look at it more closely when it slipped out of my hands. I didn't want it to fall so I grabbed for it as quickly as I could. I caught it all right—but I squeezed it too tight. Blop! What a sticky, gooey mess all over my hands and dress! Mama just shook her head with a smile and helped me clean up.

Sometimes, a mother hen would lay a whole nest full of eggs. Then she would sit on them faithfully until the eggs hatched into tiny, fluffy, yellow baby chicks. I loved to watch the whole family go chirping and cheeping across the yard. The mother hen clucked and called her family, watching over them carefully. If another animal came near, she would cluck at it angrily, then lead her chicks to safety in the barn.

Whenever there was a family of bright yellow chicks in the barn, Daddy would pick up one of the fluffy little peepers and put it in my hands to hold. I loved to feel their soft, beautiful feathers.

Once when I was alone in the barnyard watching a family of chicks go by with their mother, I reached down to pick up a fluffy chick. It started peeping loudly, and the mother hen was upset. She puffed out her feathers and ran straight at me, making angry clucking sounds. I screamed and ran away as fast as my legs would go!

A small creek ran beside our house, and Virgil and I loved to play hide-and-seek behind the big boulders where the water ran. It didn't matter if my feet got wet because I always went barefoot anyway.

It wasn't always safe to play in our stream. Sometimes, when the rain fell for days and days, our little stream turned into a rushing flood that could knock a person down and carry them away.

When that happened, the roaring water was so loud you could hear it everywhere. I had a hard time going to sleep at night when the creek was so loud. I would lie awake in my dark room and imagine scary things. Then I would creep out of my bed, push back the curtains over my window, and try to see if the swirling water was out of its banks. I was afraid that the flood would push our house downstream. Frightened, I would run to my daddy's bed.

He would scoop me up in one strong arm. "Don't be afraid, little one," he always said as he tucked me back in bed. Once in a while, if I was really frightened, he would put me in the big bed between him and Mama. That was a wonderful place to sleep on a rainy, scary night.

The first thing I can remember when I was little was one time when my daddy stood me on the kitchen table, held out his arms, and told me to jump into them.

I jumped right into his safe, strong arms.

Again and again, he said, "Jump, little one." After each jump, he would take another step away from the table so I would have to jump farther. I kept jumping, and he always caught me in his safe strong arms. Then he would toss me into the air toward the ceiling while I laughed and squealed.

One Friday afternoon, Mama washed my hair as usual. Then she made curls on her fingers. We didn't have fancy curlers and hair spray like we have today. She would dip her brush in sugared water and then brush each curl around her finger. It was very important that I hold my wiggly head still while the curls dried, so she put my little red chair on top of the table for me to sit in.

It was fun sitting high up on the table. I was as tall as the grown-ups! One time, the door opened and in came my daddy. I forgot all about my drying curls, I knew just what to do for fun. Quick as a flash, I leaped into the air toward him.

But my daddy had not even seen me on the table. Can you imagine what happened next?

No one caught me. I hit the hard floor with a crash-bang! Can you imagine me crying with disappointment and pain?

My surprised father picked me up tenderly. My mother kissed the bruises all better. My brother said, "What a stupid thing to do!"

Yes, it was, but I never made that mistake again. Never!

2

Pansy Faces

What I liked most about living in our little brown house was that we were near my Grandpa Willie's family and near my great-grandma Ellen White. If I walked out our front gate and turned to the right, it took about five minutes to walk up the hill to Grandpa Willie's big white house. But if I went out the gate and turned left, I could walk across the wooden bridge over the creek, past the big barn, and in only three or four minutes, I could be at Grandma Ellen's house. She named it Elmshaven.

One morning, my mother helped me

pick a handful of our prettiest pansies from our flower garden. Then she let me take them to Grandma Ellen and visit her all by myself. I felt very grown up. Auntie Sara, who lived with Grandma Ellen and helped take care of her, opened the door for me. Sara McEnterfer wasn't really our aunt, but that's what we all called her. She let me go through the front room and up the beautiful red-carpeted stairs. At the top of the stairs, I ran down the long hall and into Grandma's writing room.

When Grandma Ellen saw me, her face turned into one big smile. She pushed her flat writing board to the side of her chair and held out her arms. I ran straight into them.

Grandma Ellen spent time every day writing down the things God showed her and told her. She was a messenger for God. He gave her wonderful dreams called visions. Sometimes, angels came and spoke to her.

This morning, she hugged me tightly and thanked me as she took the flowers from my grimy little hand. She smiled like I had given her the biggest bouquet of flowers from a real flower shop!

"Look at all these smiling pansy faces!" Grandma Ellen said with a laugh. "That's why pansies are one of my favorite flowers. They make me happy. Look, Mabel! Every pansy is smiling at you."

I had never thought of pansies having faces. Suddenly, I could see their faces too!

"Mabel," Grandma Ellen said, "point to a pansy face that looks sad or mean."

I looked carefully at each flower. "Grandma, there are no sad faces. Every pansy is smiling."

Grandma Ellen smiled. "That's why I like pansies. They make me happy, because they are happy." She pulled me closer. "Jesus wants us to be like pansies. He wants us to bring happiness to everyone around us."

I liked talking with my Grandma Ellen. "Mabel," she asked, "do you know what pansies do the very first thing in the morning?"

I shook my head. "No. What do they do?"

"The first thing a pansy does in the morning is turn its face toward the sun," she said. "It needs light and warmth to make it grow. All day long, that pansy keeps its face toward the sun as the sun slowly crosses the sky. Then when the sun sets and it gets dark, the pansy rests all night, trusting that the sun will wake it up again the next morning.

"Mabel, Jesus wants us to be like pansies," she said. "He keeps us safe all night and wakes us up in the morning. Jesus is our bright, warm, loving Sun. 'Thank You, dear Jesus,' we say when we wake up and think about Him. 'Thank You for Your love and care. I give myself to You this morning. Help me be happy and obedient all day.'"

Grandma squeezed my hand. "All your life, Mabel, remember to talk with Jesus the moment you wake up and start a new day. Ask Jesus to be with you all that day. He loves you so much that He will never leave you. If you're tempted to do something wrong, remember that He is only a whisper away. You can say, 'Dear Jesus, please help me to be true and loyal to You.' Never forget, Mabel, that He can even hear the prayers you whisper in your own mind."

And I have remembered what my Grandma Ellen told me that day. It was more than eighty years ago now, but whenever I see a pansy, I remember to smile. And I have learned during the years of my life that what Grandma Ellen said is true. If I talk to my Heavenly Father when I first wake up, and ask Him to help me do the right things through the day, He always does. He helps me grow more and more like Jesus.

Chapter 3

How We Got There

How did it happen that my family was living in that little brown house when I was born? I'll tell you!

For many years, my great-grandmother Ellen White and my great-grandfather James White worked hard to help our small church—the Seventh-day Adventist Church—grow. They were worn out from all the hard work and travel—which wasn't easy in those days. They traveled mostly on horseback or in carriages, and it took weeks and weeks to go all the places they visited.

By then, James and Ellen White had two married sons, Edson and Willie. But James never got to see any of his grandchildren. Two days after he turned sixty years old, James White died. A few months later, Willie and his wife, Mary, had a baby girl they named Ella May White. Twenty-eight years later she became my mother. Grandma Ellen loved the new grandbaby and never forgot that the first word baby Ella ever spoke was "Gamma."

When Ella was eight years old and her little sister Mabel was only three, a very sad thing happened. Their beautiful mother died. Grandma Ellen opened her heart and her home to these two grandchildren. They moved in to live in her house. In fact, for the rest of Grandma Ellen's life, their families either lived together or next door to each other.

Before long, Grandma Ellen and all of her family and helpers sailed in a boat to Australia. For nine years they lived there and worked to help the church in Australia grow. They helped start a college and a hospital.

Willie White was in charge of all the church in Australia in those years. He was very busy but very lonely without a wife. But one day, he met a lovely young woman named Ethel May Lacey, and before long, they fell in love.

"I asked her to marry me," Willie told his mother.

"Oh, Willie," Grandma Ellen said, "I hope she said yes!"

Willie shook his head. "I'm leaving on a trip to New Zealand, and I'll be gone for several months. I told her that knowing she loved me and wanted to marry me would make me very happy. She said, 'Pray about it while you are gone. I cannot give you my answer now. I'll have an answer when you return.' So I have to wait."

So Willie left, and he waited for Ethel May's answer. But Grandma Ellen didn't have to wait as long. One day, Ethel May told her, "The Lord has given me my answer. I know that it is God's plan for me to marry Willie."

Grandma Ellen was very happy to know

that her son would have a gentle, loving wife. Ethel May was very welcome in the White family. Grandma Ellen wrote in a letter to her son Edson, "She is exactly the right person for Willie. Wherever Ethel May is, there you will find sunshine and love."

The years went by, and it was time for the Whites to return to America. When Grandma Ellen moved to Australia, she had only two grandchildren—Ella and Mabel. Now she had five. Willie and Ethel May had twin boys—Henry and Herbert, four years old, and a tiny new baby named Grace. By now, Mabel was thirteen, and Ella was all grown up at eighteen years old.

The family spent three weeks sailing across the Pacific Ocean toward home. Several times on the voyage, God talked with Grandma Ellen in visions. Visions are like dreams, except you're not asleep. It's a very special way that God uses to talk with special people like my Grandma Ellen. On the boat, she asked God, "Where should I make my home in America?"

His answer was that He had a special quiet place waiting for her where she could rest and write. Even though Grandma Ellen was almost seventy-three years old, God still had many things for her to write about.

But God didn't tell her where this special place was. She and Willie decided that it must be in California, near Pacific Press, where many of her books were being printed.

So on a Monday morning after the family's boat had docked in San Francisco, they started hunting for a house big enough for all of them. That wasn't easy to find! And they had left all their furniture and things in Australia. It would have cost too much money to bring it all with them on the ship. They had very little money.

The family looked all over the city. The houses for sale were either too small or they cost too much money. All day Monday, Tuesday, and Wednesday they searched. Finally, Grandma Ellen said, "The Lord told me that He has a quiet place ready for us. I shall wait for Him to show us where."

Willie could see that his mother was tired. "Mother," he suggested, "why don't you and Sara (Grandma Ellen's helper and nurse) take the train to St. Helena Sanitarium (a big building like a hospital, only people often went there even if they weren't sick just to rest) up in the Napa Valley. It's only about sixty miles away. You can rest there while I keep looking for a house."

"Good idea," Grandma Ellen said with a smile. On that Thursday, she and Sara left on the train for St. Helena.

The next day, Friday, Grandma Ellen met an old friend who told her about a large house that was for sale only a short distance down the hill from the Sanitarium. The house was to be sold with everything in it. Grandma Ellen agreed to go and look at it. "But I know we can never, never afford such a beautiful, expensive house."

Grandma Ellen and her friend were shown through the large, two-story house. There were carpets on the floors and curtains on the windows. Every room had just the right furniture—tables, beds, and chairs. The closets were filled with sheets, towels, tablecloths—everything a house needed. The kitchen shelves held dishes, pots, and pans. Firewood was stacked in place to burn in the big black cook stove or in one of the three fireplaces.

Outside, they found vegetables growing in a garden, ready to pick and eat. There were ripe grapes on vines and hundreds of fruit and olive trees. Down by the creek was an orchard—two thousand prune trees. In the barn, they found hens laying eggs and a cow giving milk to her calf.

Two beautiful horses trotted up to be petted. Grandma Ellen loved horses. Horses had taken her many thousands of miles in her traveling work for God. She saw a big farm wagon, four carriages, and tons of hay for the animals. The thought of ever owning a lovely country home like this one seemed like an impossible dream.

Finally, she asked, "What is the selling price of this house?"

The answer was God's exciting surprise. The price was so low that they could buy it with the money they had! Right away, Grandma Ellen knew that this was the quiet place God had promised her.

Can you imagine the fun she had sending a message back to her family in Oakland? "Stop hunting for a house! Pack your things and come on up. I've found our house and I'm buying it!" Quickly they came.

The family was so surprised to see that their new home was already filled with all the furniture they needed. Now there was no need to go and buy new beds or tables or couches or anything.

They brought only a few things back with them from Australia. One of those was Grandma Ellen's writing chair. This comfortable chair had a flat board attached to one side. Grandma Ellen put her papers on this flat board when she was writing. When she was ready to stand up, the board swung out of her way to the side.

That night she wrote, "I never dreamed of ever owning such a perfect home on this earth." Again and again, she thanked her heavenly Father for such a quiet place in which to live and write for Him.

She called her new home Elmshaven, because of the elm trees that grew in the yard.

The very next day after they were moved in, Grandma Ellen was busy writing down God's messages. Her work became busier and busier. People wanted her to visit them, to speak to them, to come to their meetings. She needed more help.

A young man who had helped her in Australia was hired to help her with her writing work. His name was Dores E. Robinson. He lived at Elmshaven and ate meals with the family. Of course, he met Grandma Ellen's granddaughter Ella. During the next few years, their friendship turned into love.

Ella's father, Willie White, married them in the Sanitarium church the next summer. Grandma Ellen offered the special prayer for the bride and groom.

For the next five years, Ella and Dores lived in father Willie White's large house.

It was here that Virgil, my brother, was born—in the same room where his uncle Arthur White had been born only three months before.

At last, Ella and Dores were able to save enough money to build a little brown house on the land Grandama Ellen had given them.

I was born in that little brown house even before the paint Daddy was putting on the doors had time to dry.

Chapter

4

Virgil's Marble

One Friday morning, I climbed up on a chair to watch Mama pile chocolate frosting on a cake she had just baked. "Mabel, tomorrow is your brother's birthday," she said. "Birthdays and birthday cakes are very special."

I stared as she placed the candles on the cake, including a bright red one for the center. "We are getting everything ready today, because tomorrow is Sabbath. We will give Virgil his gifts today so he can play with them this afternoon. We'll have the cake tomorrow."

While Mama put the cake pans in the sink, I stood beside the cake. Oh, how I wanted to stick my finger in for a tiny taste. But I knew I shouldn't. Mama must have known what I was thinking. Quickly she came back and covered the cake and hid it in the cupboard. "Let's keep this cake a secret," she said. "We want to surprise Virgil with it."

At noon that day, Daddy came home from his office for lunch. After we ate our food, we sang, "Happy birthday, dear Virgil." Then Daddy handed him three wrapped presents. Virgil ripped the paper off his first gift in a hurry. It was a singing top—a toy he had wanted for a long time. He wound it up and sent it merrily spinning and humming across the kitchen floor.

Virgil tore open his next present. It was a pair of warm mittens. "Thanks!" he called as he reached for the last package. When the paper was off of that one, his eyes lit up with joy. It was a big, beautiful glass marble!

Virgil collected marbles. Daddy had taught him how to play marbles by drawing a circle in the dirt and putting the marbles inside. Then he'd take an extra marble, hold it between his thumb and finger, and flick it at the other marbles to knock one out of the circle.

I didn't get to play marbles, but I liked to watch. Every marble was so pretty, each one with a different swirl of colors. I wasn't allowed to even touch them because Mama was afraid I would put one in my mouth, swallow it and choke.

But this new marble was different. It was big, too big to go in my mouth. "Virgil," Mama said, "Let Mabel hold your birthday marble." Oh, was I ever excited!

When Virgil was ready to share, I held my hands together and he dropped the marble into them. I just stared at it. Streaks of blue, red and yellow swirled around inside it. Right in the center, there was a red flower shape. The petals seemed to move when I rolled the marble.

I thought it was the prettiest thing I had ever seen. I wanted to keep it. When Virgil asked for it back, I shook my head.

"Mabel," he said, "give me my marble."

I just held it tighter and said, "No."

"Mama," he shouted, "Mabel won't give me my marble."

"Ask her again, gently," Mama suggested.

He tried. "Please give me my marble. It's my birthday present."

"No!" I shouted.

"Little One," Daddy said in a surprised voice, "Virgil let you hold it. Now thank him and hand the marble back."

I felt the smooth marble in my hand and stared at the sparkling colors. Give it back? "No, no!" I cried.

My shocked parents glanced at each other. Then Mama's head nodded. Papa picked up my little red chair and placed it near the kitchen door. Then he picked me up while I held tightly to the marble and set me down in my chair. "Little One," he said kindly but firmly, "you must sit in this chair until you choose to give Virgil his marble."

I sat in my little red chair all afternoon.

Every so often, when Mama wasn't looking, my brother poked his head around the door and stuck his tongue out at me. Would I give him the marble? No!

When supper time came, Mama brought a bowl of warm bread and milk to me in my chair. That's all I had to eat while I sat there and watched my family talk, laugh, and eat my favorite soup, sandwiches, cherries, and cookies.

"We miss you, Mabel," Daddy called. "Come on over. Give Virgil his marble. This supper is oh, so good."

It sounded and smelled very good—much better than my bread and milk. But give up this marble? No!

As the sun was going down that Friday evening, Mama played the organ to welcome Sabbath. Daddy picked up my chair and set me near the organ. Mama said with a smile. "Sing with us, Mabel." I didn't feel like singing. I knew I was being bad. Finally, I fell asleep in my chair while Daddy was reading a story.

The next thing I knew, I was in my

cozy bed and it was Sabbath morning. When I opened my eyes, my room was filled with bright yellow sunshine and right above me was Mama's loving face. "Jump up, Mabel," she said with a kiss. "Let's put on your Sabbath clothes. We'll have breakfast and then off to Sabbath School we'll go!"

I jumped up happily. I loved Sabbath School! When Mama and I walked to the kitchen, she put the pretty glass marble in my hands and said, "Give this to Virgil, then climb up in your chair for breakfast."

Still smiling, I ran to where Virgil sat at the table to give him his marble. Suddenly I remembered. All my happiness disappeared. I stopped in the middle of the floor.

"Hurry, Little One," Daddy called. "Your peach toast is getting cold."

I gazed at the pretty marble in my hands. The longer I looked at it, the louder the voice inside me said, Keep it. I will keep it, I decided. Virgil was holding out his hand. I looked at him and shook my head. "No. I want it."

"Mabel," Daddy said in a disappointed voice, "Go sit in your chair and stay there until you choose to obey." I went to my chair. Mama brought me a bowl of warm bread and milk.

A few minutes later, I heard the rich, silvery bell of the St. Helena Sanitarium Church ring out over the valley. It was ringing, "Time to come to Sabbath School." I watched as Virgil and Daddy headed out the door. Oh, how I wanted to go! Stubbornly I chose to disobey and keep my brother's marble and sit in my little red chair all morning.

Mama stayed home with me. She didn't scold me or nag at me. She just talked about Jesus, about how He always chose to obey His parents and His heavenly Father. Mama prayed with me. She asked Jesus to help me be obedient.

I sat in my chair all that long, long morning. My legs ached to get up and run. At last Daddy and Virgil came home. Mama put Virgil's wonderful birthday dinner and cake on the table. Again, she invited me to give up the marble and come eat with them.

I shook my head and held the marble tightly. I was given another bowl of warm bread and milk. I didn't want it. I hated it. On the table was mashed potatoes and gravy. I could smell the baked beans and see the chocolate cake. Was choosing to disobey and keep Virgil's marble worth eating bread and milk again?

All at once, I jumped up, ran to my brother and handed him his marble. He didn't laugh at me or make me feel bad. "Thank you, little sister," he said as he gave me a hug. Daddy and Mama clapped their hands.

"This is how happy Jesus and the angels feel every time we choose to do right," Mama said happily. And then we all sat down together, one big happy family celebrating Virgil's birthday. The cat enjoyed my bread and milk while I enjoyed a piece of the birthday cake. Deep down inside, I was very glad that I had chosen to obey.

Many years later I asked my father, "Why did you put up with such a stubborn little girl? You were strong enough to take the marble from my hand and force me to obey."

I will always remember what he said. "God never forces us to obey Him though He is strong enough. The only obedience He accepts comes from a loving heart that chooses to do right."

Today I am thankful that my parents wisely knew that if I learned to choose to obey them when I was small, I would know how to choose to obey my heavenly Father when I grew older.

Chapter
5

Writing for God

Ding-dong! Ding-dong!

I heard the Elmshaven dinner bell ring while I was playing in the yard of our little brown house. I knew that in a few minutes I would see my father walk down the road, over the bridge, and through our gate.

"Mama," I called, "may I run to meet Daddy?"

"Yes, dear," she answered cheerfully. Mama never had to warn me to look both ways before I crossed the road because only one or two people in our little valley even owned an automobile. Oh, how I wished for a ride in one!

After I got outside our gate, I began to run. If I could get to the office before Daddy left, I might be able to watch him make words on his huge black typewriter. I was proud of my Daddy. His father, Asa T. Robinson—I called him Grandpa Robinson—told me that when Daddy was only nine years old, he learned to write in a special code called shorthand. He wanted to learn so he could write fast enough to copy down every word of Grandpa's sermons.

Grandpa Robinson told me about the time that Grandma Ellen asked him if he knew someone who could write shorthand and type on a typewriter. She needed someone to write down her sermons and talks and help her with writing her books.

"Yes," my grandpa answered. "My son, Dores, has been writing down my sermons in shorthand and typing them out ever since he was ten years old." And that's how my father began working for Grandma Ellen. He was only eighteen years old then.

Why did Grandma Ellen need people to help her with her writing? I already told you that when she was seventeen, God asked her to be a special messenger to His people. During the rest of her life, God gave her more than two thousand visions. "Write! Write! Write!" her angel kept saying to her. So she did. She wrote for God. When she died in 1915, she had written more than any other woman in history!

And writing was not easy for her. She was often sick. Her hand shook and hurt. She didn't use a computer or even a type-writer. She didn't even have a pen like we have today. The pen she used had to be dipped into a bottle of ink. After she wrote three or four words, she would have to dip it in again. That ink could be very messy!

But God wanted her to keep everything she wrote or said in her sermons. And there weren't any tape recorders or video cameras. So she hired people like my daddy to travel with her and write down all the things she said. Then he would type all the things she said and all the things she wrote by hand.

To keep Grandma Ellen's writings safe, Grandpa Willie had a fireproof room built at the back of the Elmshaven office. It had huge iron doors and locks, but no windows. All the messages that God gave Grandma Ellen were kept safely there. Today, they are kept in fireproof rooms in the offices of the White Estate.

In those rooms there are two thousand sheets of Grandma Ellen's own handwriting. There are three thousand typed sermons and talks and diary pages. More than five thousand magazine articles and five thousand letters she wrote are there too. God has protected those messages all these years so we would still have them today. Her writings have been translated into more than 140 languages. And not one word in all of her 125 books disagrees with God's Holy Bible.

God often spoke to Grandma Ellen during the night. Sometimes He sent an angel choir to sing to her. He showed her things in visions that would happen in the future, before Jesus returns. She even saw heaven in her visions!

Grandma Ellen often woke up about three o'clock in the morning. All of Elmshaven was quiet and dark and she knew she could write without being interrupted. She would put on her warm robe and walk down the hall to her writing room carrying her lighted kerosene lamp. She would strike a match and light a fire in the fireplace which Auntie Sara always had ready for her.

Then for three or four hours, she sat in her little rocking chair with her bottle of ink, her pen, and paper on her lapboard. With angels all around her, she wrote down the things that God had shown her.

At seven o'clock, the Elmshaven bell would ring. Grandma Ellen would lay down her pen and join her family of workers for worship and breakfast. After breakfast, she usually took a nap for a few hours. When she woke up, Auntie Sara would give her treatments if she was sick or in pain, then take her for a horse and buggy ride in the fresh air.

On this day, I was running to meet Daddy before he left his office. When I got to the yard at the back of Elmshaven, there was my father talking with Grandma Ellen. I ran to hold his hand.

Grandma Ellen smiled at me. "Mabel, would you like to go for a buggy ride with me after dinner?"

Would I? "Oh, yes, yes, yes, Grandma!"

Grandma Ellen smiled again. "Sara will stop the horse at your gate to pick her up," she told Daddy.

I could hardly wait for dinner!

6

A Buggy Ride With Grandma Ellen

At the dinner table that noon, Mama didn't have to say, "Mabel, stop playing with your food. Eat your dinner." For once, I didn't need anyone to tell me to hurry. Grandma Ellen had promised to stop right after dinner and take me on her horse and buggy ride. Long before I heard the clip-clop of the horse's hooves on the gravel road, my face and hands were clean, and I was swinging on our front gate, waiting.

"Here they come," I called as Auntie Sara pulled the horse up to our gate. Mama was there in a moment to lift me up into the buggy. She whispered in my ear, "Remember, Grandma Ellen may be tired. Don't wiggle and don't chatter all the time."

"I won't," I promised.

Grandma Ellen put me in the middle between her and Auntie Sara. I really wanted to sit on the outside, but Grandma was afraid I might fall out on the wheel. The buggy didn't have a step like most buggies did because Grandma Ellen could not lift herself up on the step and into the buggy. To help her get in, they took the railing off one end of the porch. Then they could drive the buggy right up to the porch. All Grandma had to do was step from the porch into the buggy.

Grandma Ellen put her arm around me, pulled me close and gave me a little squeeze. I still remember how cozy and warm I felt, all tucked in next to her.

"We are going to drive around Glass Mountain," Grandma told me. That was the name of the little mountain next to our house. "I want to see a new family who moved into the little house on the other

side. They haven't had time to plant any vegetables yet, so we are taking them these ripe
tomatoes and green beans."

That was just like my Grandma Ellen,
always doing something thoughtful for others. We drove by little farm houses along
Glass Mountain Road. If anyone was outside, they waved to us and we waved back
to them.

Several times, Auntie Sara stopped the
horse so Grandma could talk with someone.
Some of these people didn't even know that
Grandma's name was Ellen White. They
only knew her as "the little old lady who
loves Jesus."

Grandma said something nice to me
about each person she waved to or spoke
with. No wonder strangers were friendly
and quickly learned to love her.

After I grew up, I often wondered why I
loved my great-grandmother so much. I was
young and busy all the time and she was
old and weak. Why did I like to be around
her so much?

I think I found the answer in a letter that

Auntie Sara wrote to my grandpa Willie back in those days. She wrote, "Your mother's health has been more than we dared hope for during your absence. She sings in the night. She sings in the day and even while in the bathtub while taking her treatment. We get her out to ride twice nearly every day."

What child wouldn't love a sweet grandma who sings in the night, sings in the day, and even sings in the bathtub?

Chapter

7

Prunes! Prunes! Prunes!

"Look, they're plowing under the prune trees! Only another day or two of school, and then we'll be out to pick up the prunes!" Excited children shouted and pointed as they made their way down the Sanitarium hill to the Foothill schoolhouse.

"Last year, I picked ten boxes a day," claimed an eighth-grade boy.

"I can do better than that," bragged a younger boy.

"Please," begged the girls, "don't work that fast. As soon as all the prunes are picked up, we'll have to go back to school."

The boys shook their heads. "That's not important. Think of all the money we can earn—ten cents a box. We're going to work so fast that you girls will be left in the dust!"

When Grandma Ellen bought Elmshaven, there was a orchard of two thousand prune trees on the land. Each year when the prunes were ready to pick, Mr. James, her farmer, would plow under the trees, then rake the ground smooth and soft. Then strong boxes were piled high at the end of each row of trees. When everything was ready, strong farm men went into the orchard and shook the trees. Ripe prunes would fall like rain down to the soft ground.

Every year, the Foothill School was closed while the students went to pick prunes. This way, they could earn money to help pay for their school bills.

There had been no church school for the children whose parents worked at the St. Helena Sanitarium before Grandma Ellen arrived. But one of the first things she did after buying Elmshaven was to give the church land on which to build a ten-grade school. In 1902, the school opened.

Five of Grandma Ellen's grandchildren and a dozen of her great-grandchildren went to the Foothill School. I remember walking down the path through our goat pasture, across the Sanitarium road, and on to the schoolyard. It took only five minutes from my house.

I didn't like prune time. Everyone had to work to pick the prunes—even me! Oh, how I hated getting down in the dirt on my hands and knees to pick them up. I hated the feel of dirt under my fingernails—sometimes I think I can still feel it. I wonder if I ever filled even one box of prunes. What I really wanted was a girl my own age to work and play with, but there was no one.

Virgil had three friends. Our uncle, Arthur White, was nearly his same age, as were Donald Bree and Lloyd Mason. Their parents worked for Grandma Ellen also. These boys were excited about earning money. I just wanted to run and hide.

Sometimes I helped my aunt Grace. She

was fourteen, and her job was to keep a bucket filled with cool lemonade for any of the pickers who were thirsty. And it was fun to watch Mr. James and his helpers dump the prunes into huge wire baskets and the dip them in boiling liquid. This cracked the skins. Then the prunes were set out on tables to dry in the sun for a few days.

To Grandma Ellen, every prune was precious. God made it grow. It was food and we knew it was a sin to waste food when people were hungry. So when all those prunes were picked, dried, and packed into boxes, Grandma Ellen gave them away. She gave tons of prunes to Adventist schools where students were hungry, and many were shipped overseas to missionaries.

8

Never Too Busy to Love Us

When Grandma Ellen was nearly eighty-seven years old, she and her helpers worked extra long hours. They were trying to finish her last book about the Bible. Since Grandma Ellen was so old, they were afraid she might not live very much longer.

Even my mother was helping in the office. Virgil and I played in the yard around Elmshaven so she could keep an eye on us through the windows.

I was lonely with everyone so busy. No one had time for me—no one, that is, but

Grandma Ellen. She always had time to talk to us children. The hard part was getting to see her. And that was because of Auntie Sara.

If she saw us near the back door, the door we always went in, she would say, "You children run and play. Your Grandma is busy." Virgil and I never, ever disobeyed Auntie Sara. She was Grandma's nurse and helper for thirty years, and she seemed to be in charge of Elmshaven.

One day my brother, who was always thinking up things to do, said, "If Auntie Sara doesn't see us, she can't say, 'Don't bother your Grandma.' Let's play in the front of the house today."

Of course, there was a front door, but we never went in that way unless our parents were with us.

A long time later that day, we saw Auntie Sara drive away with the horse and buggy, going to town for something. In a flash, Virgil grabbed my hand and we ran for the back porch. Grandma's writing room was directly above the kitchen. We went in through the back door and across the porch to the back stairs to her room.

Those stairs scared me. They were steep, narrow and dark, with only one tiny window for light. But Virgil wasn't afraid. He was never afraid of anything. He almost pulled me up those spooky stairs to a tiny door that opened into Grandma's writing room.

We knew Grandma Ellen was a special person and that we shouldn't pester her. So when Virgil opened the little door to her room, we stood and waited quietly for her to see us. She was sitting across the room in her favorite writing place, a spot with windows on three sides.

When she looked up, she smiled and said, "Come on over."

Bubbling with happiness, I ran across that big room to the side of her chair. She was too old and I was too big to sit on her lap. But when she put one arm around me and one arm around Virgil, we knew that she loved us. She listened as we told her what we had been doing that morning. She was always interested in what we said.

Maybe this was the time when Grandma Ellen took both of my hands in hers, kissed them and said, "These pretty little hands belong to you and to Jesus. Ask Jesus and He will help these hands do thousands of thoughtful, loving things before they grow old."

Then she asked us to think of something we could do that very day that would help Mama and Daddy. Virgil said he would sweep the front porch and steps of our little brown house. I said I could put the silverware on the table.

"Good!" Grandma said. "Try and remember to do it before your mother asks you to. Surprise her!"

Then she thought of something else we could do. "Your mother is busy helping me in the office," she said. "Would you like to help her by picking a basket of peas from the garden?"

"Yes! Yes, Grandma!" we answered.

"Ask the cook in the kitchen for a basket," she said. Then we happily ran back down the stairs. Happy for something helpful to do. Happy for a grandma who was never too busy to love us.

9

Birthdays, Baseball, and Automobiles

Some of my happiest memories of living at Elmshaven near Grandma Ellen are my birthday parties.

When my mother, Ella, was a little girl only eight years old, her mother died. Grandma Ellen opened her arms and took Ella and her sister Mabel into her home. Years later in Australia, her father married a young and lovely woman named Ethel May Lacey. She was only eight years older than my mother. So when Virgil and I were born, she was too young to be a grandmother. She asked us to call her "Mama

White." Virgil and I always did. We loved her very much.

Every year, Mama White planned a birthday party for me and her two youngest boys, Arthur and Frances. Our birthdays were only a few days apart. As I mentioned before, Arthur was the same age as Virgil, and Frances was three years younger than me. Mama White always gave us an ice cream party—a special treat.

My twin uncles, Henry and Herbert, bought a huge block of ice from the Sanitarium store and brought it all the way down the hill in our little red wagon. While they were gone, Mama White cooked a custard, cooled it, and put it in the ice-cream container.

When they got home, the twins smashed the block of ice on the cellar steps. Then they mixed some salt in with the ice and packed it around the ice-cream container. When the crank handle of the ice-cream maker was turned, the container would spin around in the ice and the custard inside was whipped by special blades.

At first, even I could turn the ice-cream crank. But as the custard inside got colder, it started to freeze and it took the strong arms of the twins to turn it. And when they couldn't turn it another time, it was time to call, "It's frozen!" Suddenly, out of nowhere, everyone appeared on the cellar steps hoping for just a little tiny taste of the ice cream.

We usually had the birthday party outside around the picnic table under the trees. Mama would bring the cake. Sometimes we needed two cakes, because when everyone showed up, there were more than a dozen of us!

When Grandma Ellen was too sick or weak to join us outside, we always took a piece of the birthday cake to her.

Another time I remember being very special was Sabbath. My father was the pastor at the church nearby in a town called Calistoga. We rode there in our buggy pulled by our horse named Babe. We had to leave very early if we wanted to be on time for Sabbath School. And we always wanted to be on time. Since Daddy was the pastor, he wanted to set a good example.

Daddy was one of the first people to arrive at church every week. And he was always the last one to leave. I had to learn not to hang onto his hand pulling and saying, "Let's go."

Just like you, we were always hungry after church. And it was a long way home. But my mother always had a lunch hidden away in the buggy. When we finally left church, Daddy would drive down the road until he came to our favorite grassy spot beside a cool stream of clear water. Then he would unharness Babe and make sure she had some nice grass or hay to eat.

And Mama would let us help spread out a blanket, then bring out the basketful of food. Doesn't food always taste better when you eat it outside instead of at the dining table? Ours always did.

After lunch, our parents stretched out for a little rest. Virgil and I waded quietly in the stream. We usually remembered that it was Sabbath and played quietly. Usually we remembered, but not the time Virgil caught a water dog—that's what we called a salamander—and tried to put it down the back of my dress. You can guess what happened. I didn't feel bad when Mama made him sit on a log for a long time.

Later, we took a short walk in the woods. Then before we rode home, Mama and Daddy would read stories to us from *Our Little Friend.*

Another happy memory was when the family played baseball together. Grandma Ellen had given her grandchildren a piece of level land with the understanding that it would be used for a baseball field. Sometimes on a warm summer afternoon, someone would say, "Let's play ball tonight!" Then everyone who wanted to play got busy.

In our home, I helped Mama bake fresh bread and make sandwiches. Mama White might bake nut-and-raisin cookies, gather fresh fruit from the orchard, and bring plenty of cool milk to drink. I remember once that Grace and Arthur brought a big bowl of ripe, sweet strawberries. We ate them one by one with our fingers.

Once in a while, when the day was especially beautiful and warm, someone would go and get Grandma Ellen and Auntie Sara. They put blankets in Grandma's chair to make it warm and comfy.

Grandma Ellen said that boys and girls should learn to hit a ball. I can still see my daddy showing Virgil and Arthur how to hold and swing the bat. The older players were even patient enough to let me have a turn.

And whenever anyone hit the ball, Grandma Ellen would laugh and clap her hands.

I remember the day Virgil burst into our house, all out of breath from running. He banged the screen door shut and shouted, "Henry and Herbert bought an automobile! It's a beautiful black Model-T Ford. They promised to take Arthur and me for a ride one of these days."

He barely stopped to breathe. "Daddy, we need an automobile. Please get one. I know I could learn to drive it. Really I could!"

Daddy's answer came with a smile. "You know, when Henry and Herbert asked their father to buy a car, he told them that they could buy one—as soon as they earned enough money to pay for it. Every penny they spent on that car, they earned with hard work. So, Virgil, as soon as you can buy an automobile with your own money, it's yours."

Virgil knew that would take a long time. But he kept dreaming and saving the money he earned. And when he was nineteen years old, he bought his very first car.

One of the first people to go for a ride in Henry and Herbert's car was Grandma Ellen. She was happy for them and wrote to a friend in a letter: "Willie and his family are well. His twins are busy workers. They have recently purchased an automobile, and yesterday I took my first ride in it. It is the easiest machine I have ever ridden in."

I still remember the exciting day when our uncles took Virgil and me out on our first-ever automobile ride. They took us up the hill, past the Sanitarium, and up, up to Pacific Union College at the top of the mountain.

10

Friday Evening Memories

I shall never, ever forget Friday evenings at Elmshaven. With my Sabbath bath taken and my hair curled, I waited by our gate for Grandpa Willie's family to come by. The sun was low in the sky. We were going together for sundown worship with Grandma Ellen.

Would you have liked to go with us? This is what it would be like if you had been there. We walk along with my family—the two big boys you can't tell apart are my twin uncles, Henry and Herbert. The boy walking with Virgil is Arthur—they're always together. The pretty girl with the long brown braids is my aunt Grace. My favorite uncle is riding on Grandpa Willie's shoulders—Uncle Frances was still a baby.

We walk up the steps to the porch at Elmshaven. My father swings the front door wide open and invites us in. "It's so beautiful," you say when you see the last rays of sunlight shining through the tall stained-glass window in the stairway. Bright colors dance along the hall and into the front room.

Grandma Ellen is sitting there in her little rocking chair, happy to see us. She welcomes us to Elmshaven.

A cheery fire is burning in the fireplace. The older people sit on the couch and on the chairs, but we put pillows on the floor to sit on. The fire warms our backs.

Grace hands out the songbooks and Mother plays the little organ. We sing and sing. I look at Virgil and his eyes shout, "I can sing louder than you."

My eyes shout back, "I'll show you that you can't!"

Our voices get louder and louder and louder until we are almost screaming the words. Suddenly the music stops. I find myself looking at my father's face. What will he say?

Before he can say a word, Grandma Ellen speaks. In her gentle way, she says, "Children, someday we are going to sing with the angels. We are learning right here to join in their choir. Let's keep our voices sweet."

Sing with angels? What a thrilling thought! The others keep on singing, but all I can do is imagine singing with angels.

Grandpa Willie or Daddy reads a story from the Bible. Then we kneel for prayer and welcome in the holy Sabbath day.

When we stand up, Grandma Ellen says, "Why don't you children follow Auntie Sara into the kitchen." It was always that way at Grandma's. She didn't eat or serve supper at her house, but she knew how hungry children get, especially when Sabbath comes early.

In the kitchen we find a big bowl of sliced peaches and raisin buns still warm from

e Sara pours us each a glass of

we have to hurry back to the front
ɔm. The best part of the evening is almost
here. Every week, one of the adults tells us a
story. Tonight it is Grandma Ellen's turn.
Henry and Herbert lift up her rocker and carry
Grandma to the middle of the room. I always
push my pillow right up beside her rocker
where I can look up into her eyes and pat her
hand. I love to see her smile!

Her story starts: "One afternoon, right
here in this room, I had a long visit with
some friends. When they left, I was so tired
I went to bed early. I had a bad pain in my
left side and I couldn't rest. I kept turning
from side to side. Finally, I fell asleep.

"Later, I woke up and started to turn
again. Suddenly I realized that all my pain
was gone. I turned my hands, my arm, my
shoulder, but there was no pain. I thanked
God. Then I opened my eyes. The room was
filled with light, a most beautiful, soft, blue
light. I seemed to be in the arms of heavenly
angels.

"I sat up and saw that I was surrounded by a bright cloud that was as white as snow. Its edges were tinted with a deep pink. Sweet, soft music filled the air. I could tell that it was the singing of angels. Then a Voice spoke to me, saying, 'Fear not: I am your Savior. Holy angels are all around you.' "

"Grandma! Grandma!" we children exclaim. "Was Jesus talking to you? Jesus?"

"Yes, my dear ones," she answers. "It was Jesus, my Savior and yours. I thought I was in heaven and I cried out in joy, 'Then this is heaven. Now I can rest.'

"The Voice spoke again. 'Heaven? No, not yet. I still need you. Your work for Me is not yet done.' Then I fell asleep again. When I woke up, I heard lovely music and I wanted to sing."

Then with a burst of love, Grandma Ellen says, "Oh, children, I wish you could hear the angels singing! Someday you will. We will all sing with them around God's glorious white throne. I want you there with me to join in that choir."

"Oh, yes, Grandma," we answer. "We will be there."

We see Mother standing at the door. "Come, children," she says. "We must be up early in the morning for Sabbath School."

"Thank you, Grandma, for your story and for your love," we call over our shoulders as we go out into the dark night.

We step out into the dark and see a huge silvery moon rising over the pine trees on the hilltops. We walk home in the hush of the evening. We know that God is beside us.

11

The End . . . Until Heaven

Before many more days went by, Grandma Ellen fell down while walking to her writing room and broke her hip. After that, she wasn't able to walk anymore. She spent most of her time in bed and she got weaker and weaker. Finally, on July 16, 1915, my Grandma Ellen died.

I'll never forget her or the special ways she let me know that she loved me. One of the last times I got to visit her, she pointed to heaven and said, "I'll see you up there."

And I know that I will. Grandma Ellen was a special messenger for God and a special great-grandmother for me.

Won't you promise to meet me in heaven? I'd love to take you to meet my special Grandma Ellen.